GETTIN' READY FOR THE MIRACLE

A CHRISTMAS MUSICAL FOR YOUNG VOICES

Book and Lyrics by Linda Rebuck

Music by Tom Fettke

Lillenas Publishing Co.

KANSAS CITY, MO. 64141

Production Helps

SETTING

Very little need be done to set the stage. Much of the "setting up" will be done by choir members during the OVERTURE. The "inn door" will need to be set up ahead of time; the manger can then be placed near the inn after verse 1 of "On the Eve of the Pageant."

PROPS

Most of the props you will need are mentioned in the first song. Make sure that these props are the most visible to the audience. Additional props may be used if necessary, since every choir member should have something to carry. These are to be taken down and removed from the stage during the first 38 measures of DEPARTURE MUSIC.

BELLS—any kind will do, just to use for decorating the stage.

CLOUDS—made from cardboard or cotton batting; some may be in place before the musical begins.

ROBES—for shepherds, Mary, Joseph, three wise men, and angel.

PAGES OF MUSIC—for "eight songs for singing" line.

LARGE SHEETS OF ROLLED PAPER—for "seven scenes for painting" line.

SIX DOZEN COOKIES—in a box or other container.

HAY—glue hay to all sides of a cardboard box or large block of Styrofoam, or use a bundle of stalks for hay.

FOUR SHEPHERDS' STAFFS

THREE CROWNS FOR WISE MEN ("KINGS")

WINGS FOR ANGEL

MANGER

RING—wrapped in Christmas paper, for Katy to give to Todd.

THREE GIFTS—for wise men to carry.

CLOTH DOLL—for Sarah.

POT OR COVERED DISH—for Aaron's dinner.

LETTERS TO JESUS

PENCIL AND PAPER—for Katy to use to write her letter.

BIRTHDAY CAKE—for Katy (real or not) that is lettered "Happy Birthday, Mary."

MAIN CHARACTERS

MARY KATHERINE—outgoing, but covers her feelings of inadequacy.

GREG—absent-minded boy; the "choir clown."

MR./MRS. MARTIN—adult man or woman who is able to direct the choral group.

SHEPHERDS—three to five are needed; they should have some singing ability.

MICHAEL AND SARAH—one of shepherd's children, Sarah is very shy; Michael takes care of her.

Contents

On the Eve of the Pageant

LINDA REBUCK

Based on Traditional English Folksong
"The Twelve Days of Christmas"
Arr. by Tom Fettke

Stage is relatively empty. Risers are in place center stage.
One child enters carrying a manger. He or she walks to microphone and sings.

Verse 2: One or two more children join (carrying angels' wings).

Lyrics:
1. On the eve of the pag-eant my moth-er had to bring A man-ger for a wee king.
2. On the eve of the pag-eant our moth-ers had to bring

*Subsequent verses: each verse a few more children join, carrying the props mentioned. Add as many children on each verse as de-sired; all children need to be on stage by verse 11. Entire choir should sing from there on. (Ideally, add the number of children on each verse which corresponds with the number of props mentioned; but in most cases this is not a feasible option.)

6

8

12

Overture

Based on Traditional English Folksong
"The Twelve Days of Christmas"
Arr. by Doug Holck and Tom Fettke

During the overture, the children onstage set up the props they sang about, and the rest of the choir and cast take their places on the risers and onstage. Stage should be "set" by the finish of the overture (approx. 30 seconds).

ACTION ONSTAGE FREEZES WITH CHOIR IN PLACE.
The following scene takes place to one side—offstage, if possible—away from action onstage, to give the illusion that Mary Katherine is on her way to choir.

MARY KATHERINE:	*(out of breath)* Hi, Todd!
TODD:	*(sarcastically)* Hi, MARY CHRISTMAS!
MARY KATHERINE:	I heard you were going out of town, and I wanted to give you your Christmas gift before you go. *(She hands a package to Todd.)*
TODD:	*(speaking as he unwraps package)* Oh, that's nice of you, Mary.
MARY KATHERINE:	It's not much, but I hope you like it.
TODD:	It's . . . a ring. Looks like genuine plastic . . . the kind of ring you get for being a good little kid at the dentist's office. *(laughs)*
MARY KATHERINE:	*(showing her disappointment, but trying to smile)* It's the thought that counts, you know!
TODD:	Yeah, you're right. Thanks, Mary—have a *(exaggerated)* Merry Christmas.
MARY KATHERINE:	*(sadly)* Thanks, Todd. The same to you . . . see ya!

(Immediately after this scene, while Katy (Mary Katherine) runs backstage or down aisle for her entrance, next scene begins.)

MR. MARTIN:	Good job getting the props in place, boys and girls! Uh-oh! Someone's missing . . . don't tell me! It's Mary Rogers, isn't it?
CHOIR:	*(together)* "Yes, that's right", "Oh, not again!", etc.
MR. MARTIN:	Who stands next to you, Jamie?
JAMIE:	Sharon . . . I don't know where she is.

(Mary Katherine comes running in, out of breath. She walks over to the director, Mr. Martin.)

MARY KATHERINE (Katy):	I'm sorry I'm late again, Mr. Martin, but this time it was not my fault.
MR. MARTIN:	*(jovially)* That's what you said at the last rehearsal, when you said you were held hostage by aliens for half an hour! You'll never top that excuse. *(Kids laugh; Mary Katherine looks around at them and smiles.)* Now please take your place on the risers. We have to get started—the pageant is tomorrow night!
MARY KATHERINE:	Don't you want to know why I was late today?
MR. MARTIN:	No, that's okay; just take your place.
MARY KATHERINE:	I couldn't find Marvin.
MR. MARTIN:	WHO?
MARY KATHERINE:	Marvin . . . my pet rat. My Mom found him, though; or rather he found her! You should have heard her scream! High "C", I think! *(kids laugh)*
MR. MARTIN:	*(firmly)* Mary, take your place on the risers.
MARY KATHERINE:	My name is Katy.
MR. MARTIN:	Oh, really? You changed your name?
MARY KATHERINE:	No, it was always Katy . . . well, actually my name is Mary Katherine, but I'm tired of being called Mary.
MR. MARTIN:	Why? Mary is a nice name . . . it was Jesus' mother's name.
KATY:	*(grumpily)* Yes, I know! That's where my parents got it from! I was born on Christmas day, so they named me Mary—Mary Christmas—clever, huh?!
MR. MARTIN:	That's great, Mary—uh, I mean Katy. You get to share your birthday celebration with Jesus!
KATY:	Oh, yeah, just great! I've never had a birthday party . . . no one ever sings "Happy Birthday" to me! It's always, "We wish You a Merry Christmas" and something about 'figgy pudding' . . . whatever that is!
GREG:	AH-CHOO!
MR. MARTIN:	Bless you, Greg! Well, don't feel bad, Katy; a lot of folks forget Jesus' birthday, too. But, right now we have to begin rehearsal, so . . . *(Mimicking, Katy joins him; they say the next line together.)* "Take your place on the risers."

(Katy trips over props and makes a lot of noise as she goes to her place; she turns around and shrugs her shoulders at the director, who scowls at her; other children laugh.)

Gettin' Ready for the Miracle

LINDA REBUCK

TOM FETTKE

D.S. 3 times

(34)

be   the   Lord's first   home   on   earth, and   so   they   had   to start . . .   Get - tin'
He   will   be   the   Son   of   God,   our   Lord Em - man - u - el."
so   they watched and   wait - ed   for   Mes -   si - ah   to   ap-pear.

CODA

day!   Get - tin'   read - y   for   the mir -   a - cle,

read - y   for the mir -   a - cle,   Read - y   for the mir -   a - cle of   Christ - mas

day!   Get - tin' read - y for the mir -   a - cle,   read - y   for the mir - a - cle,

MR. MARTIN:	Nicely, done, choir. Now—Innkeeper, Mary, and Joseph, let's rehearse your scene. *(Katy starts to walk toward "inn.")*
MR. MARTIN:	Katy, where are you going?
KATY:	*(sheepishly)* You said, "Mary and Joseph!"
MR. MARTIN:	I was talking about the people playing the <u>parts</u> of Mary and Joseph!
KATY:	Oh. Well, why didn't you say so? *(A few children laugh as she goes back to her place; she enjoys the attention.)*
JOSEPH:	Mr. Martin, I can't find my staff. *(Katy rolls her eyes and looks around suspiciously.)*
MR. MARTIN:	Okay, Katy, what did you do with the staff?
KATY:	Who, me? I didn't . . .
MR. MARTIN:	Katy . . .
KATY:	*(leans over and picks up staff)* Oh, how did that get here? Here you are, Joe! *(Joseph takes the staff, shaking his head slowly. He and "Mary" walk over to the inn. The Innkeeper is behind the door. Mary and Joseph knock at the door; the door opens.)*
INNKEEPER:	Sorry, folks . . . we're all filled up . . . not a room to be had.
JOSEPH:	But, sir, if you could just find a <u>small</u> room for us. My wife is going to have a baby . . . perhaps this very night!
INNKEEPER:	Like I said, I'm sorry, but we've used up all the rooms . . . large <u>and</u> small.
JOSEPH:	Well, thank you anyway. Come, Mary. *(starts to walk away)*
INNKEEPER:	Wait just a minute! *(Joseph and Mary turn back toward him.)* There is a stable out back. It isn't much, but you're welcome to stay there if you wish.
JOSEPH AND MARY:	Oh, thank you, sir! *(They walk away to "stable" area of stage.)*

Silent Night

JOSEPH MOHR
Tr. by John F. Young, alt.

TOM FETTKE

Tenderly ♩ = ca. 88

Si - lent night! Ho - ly night!

All is calm and all is bright Round yon vir - gin moth-er and the Child.

Ho - ly in - fant, ten - der, mild, Sleep in heav - en - ly

MR. MARTIN:	The angel needs to be in place for the next scene. HEY, where is she?
GREG:	Please . . . AH-CHOO! . . . don't mention hay!
KATY:	Oh, Sharon has the chicken pox!
MR. MARTIN:	Katy, please be serious.
GREG:	Oh, I forgot! I was supposed to tell you . . . Sharon does have the chicken pox. She was supposed to bring the . . . ah-ah-ah-choo! . . . the hay.
MR. MARTIN:	Bless you, Greg! Does anyone know Sharon's part?
KATY:	*(raising her hand)* I do! I helped her learn her song.
MR. MARTIN:	Anyone else? *(pause)* No one? Katy, will you try to take the part seriously . . . no practical jokes?
KATY:	Me? Jokes? Of course not, Mr. Martin. *(She walks backstage to put on angel costume.)*
NARRATOR:	While Mary and Joseph were in Bethlehem, the time came for her baby to be born; and she gave birth to her first child, a son. She wrapped him in a blanket and laid him in a manger, because there was no room for them in the village inn. That night some shepherds were in the fields outside the village, guarding their flocks of sheep.
	(Several "shepherds"—preferably older boys from the choir—have moved to one side of the stage.)
BENJAMIN:	The stars sure are bright tonight.
AARON:	Stars? What stars? I'm starving to death, and Benjamin is star-gazing!
BENJAMIN:	Sorry, Aaron; I was just trying to change the subject from food. The stars are especially bright tonight, you know.
AARON:	Where are my children? Michael is always late, but this is the latest he's ever been! Oh, my stomach!
BENJAMIN:	If I'd known he wasn't going to come, you could have shared my dinner.
OTHER SHEPHERDS:	"Or mine", "Yes, you could have shared my dinner", etc.
JESSE:	Hey, guys, let's do something to help keep Aaron's mind off of food.
BENJAMIN:	Good idea, Jesse. Let's sing! Sing with us, Aaron; you'll forget all about being hungry.
AARON:	My growling stomach can be our music! *(start introduction to "The Heavens Are Telling")*
BENJAMIN:	How about that song that begins, "The heavens are telling the glory of God."
AARON:	You really do have a thing about stars, don't you, Ben! *(Other shepherds laugh.)*

The Heavens Are Telling

LINDA REBUCK
Based on Psalm 19

TOM FETTKE

24

I will sing prais - es to You, O_ Lord, Sing prais-es to Your ho - ly name.

I will sing prais - es to You, O Lord, Your glo - ry I will ev-er pro-claim!

2nd time to Coda

Aaron: Oh, my poor stomach!   *Jesse:* Uh-oh! Let's hit it again, guys!   **The**

D.S. al Coda

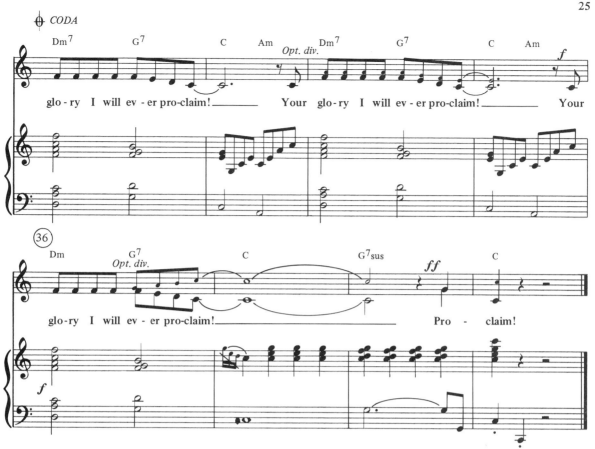

CODA

glo-ry I will ev-er pro-claim! Your glo-ry I will ev-er pro-claim! Your

glo-ry I will ev-er pro-claim! Pro - claim!

AARON:	Just wait until that boy of mine gets here. I'll . . . *(Sarah and Michael come running in. Sarah is very shy, clutches her rag doll.)*
MICHAEL:	Here's your dinner, Father.
AARON:	Michael, where <u>have</u> you <u>been</u>?
MICHAEL:	Well, I made this big pot of stew, and when I was taking it off the fire, I tripped over the dog and dropped it on the floor. But I got most of it back in the pot.
AARON:	You put the stew back in the pot after it spilled on the floor?
MICHAEL:	Well, all but the part the dog ate. *(Other shepherds laugh.)*
AARON:	I don't think I'm hungry any more.
	(Sarah has not looked at anyone; she looks down, or at her doll, at all times.)
BENJAMIN:	Hi, Sarah! How are you tonight? *(Sarah does not look up.)*
AARON:	She still hasn't spoken to anyone except that doll. It's the one her mother made just before she died.
BENJAMIN:	But that's been almost a year!
AARON:	I know. We just keep praying that she . . . *(start tape)* . . . *(Suddenly, the angel appears, interrupting the shepherds' conversation; shepherds cover their eyes and back away in fright.)*

The Angels' Message

LINDA REBUCK

TOM FETTKE

28

BENJAMIN: Come on! Let's go to Bethlehem and see the wonderful thing that has happened, that the Lord has told us about!

MICHAEL: Father, could Sarah and I come with you to see the Messiah?

AARON Yes, by all means; let's go!

(The next song is sung as the shepherds and children go to manger scene.)

We Worship Thee

LINDA REBUCK

TOM FETTKE

*4-Part Round or Unison Choir

*Notes on the preparation and performance of "We Worship Thee":

1. It may be sung as a 4-part round, unaccompanied or accompanied. Sing the song through one time in unison with full choir before singing it as a round.

2. It may be sung as a unison song with the simple accompaniment provided. Sing it through twice if performed in this manner.

3. The optional ending can be used with either of the above.

4. There is no orchestral accompaniment to this song on the tape trax. The introduction *is* included on the tape to give pitch and tempo.

Optional ending

bowed, Your__ face to __ see, We sing, we bow, we wor - ship Thee. We wor - ship Thee, O Lord.

(When song is over, all shepherds are kneeling at the manger; Michael and Sarah are standing.)

MICHAEL: Sarah, can you see the baby?

(Sarah does not answer, but looks up slowly from her doll at the Baby.)

MICHAEL: He's the Messiah, Sarah—the king God promised us.

SARAH: *(hesitantly)* Does . . . does he have a name?

MICHAEL: Yes, I heard his mother say his name is Jesus. He has come to be the Savior, and . . . Sarah! You spoke! Father, Sarah spoke!

AARON: *(Gets up, walks over to Sarah.)* What did she say?

MICHAEL: She asked if the baby had a name.

AARON: What a night! The Messiah is born, and Sarah speaks! *(kneels again)* Thank You, heavenly Father.

MICHAEL: Sarah, would you like to come with me to tell our friends about the new King?

SARAH: Uh-huh!

AARON: I want to come too, Michael. *(Aaron puts one arm around each child; they walk away.)*

SARAH: Just a minute! *(She turns around, goes back to the manger and lays her rag doll beside the Baby.)*

MICHAEL: Sarah, <u>what</u> are you <u>doing</u>?

SARAH: *(as she comes back)* I wanted to give the Baby Jesus something special, and my rag doll is the nicest thing I have.

AARON: Sarah, that is a very nice gift. You're a very special little girl. *(Sarah smiles shyly.)*

Come and Adore

LINDA REBUCK and Latin hymn
Tr. by Frederick Oakeley

TOM FETTKE and tune ADESTE FIDELIS
from Wade's CANTUS DIVERSI

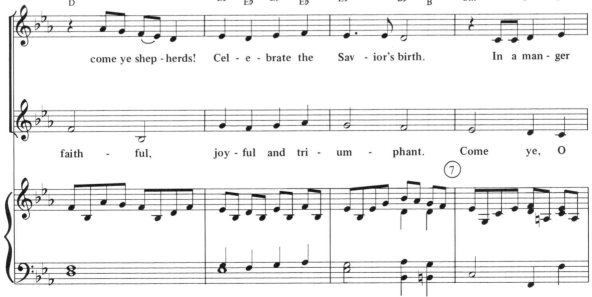

*It may be necessary to have a number of choir members sing with the congregation. Or, 2-part choir may be desirable—an even split between original and traditional song is appropriate.

11
lies the Babe, the King of heav'n and earth! Hal - le -
come ye to Beth - le - hem.
11 Come
lu - jah, hal - le - lu - jah! Kneel and wor - ship Christ the King.
and be - hold Him, born the King of an - gels. O
15
Come, a - dore, and wor - ship Him; Come, a - dore, and
come, let us a - dore Him; O come, let us a -
15

34

MR. MARTIN:	That was great, kids! Katy, you were a terrific angel!
	(Katy has been watching play intently.)
KATY:	*(looking solemn)* What? *(unenthusiastically)* Oh, thank you.
MR. MARTIN:	What's wrong, Katy?
KATY:	I just realized that Jesus was just like me. <u>He</u> didn't get many birthday presents, either!
GREG:	Speaking of gifts, (AH-CHOO!) what happened to the wise guys . . . *(other kids laugh)* . . . uh, wise men? They gave Him gold freckles and a mirror, or something. *(more laughter)*
MR. MARTIN:	Gold, frankincense, and myrrh . . . can anyone tell us what those gifts were? *(Some raise hands.)* Eric?
ERIC:	Frankincense and myrrh were sort of like perfume.
MR. MARTIN:	That's right, and does anyone know why we're doing the "wise men" scene later? *(more hands raised)* Okay, Jamie.
JAMIE:	The Bible says that the wise men came into a "house"; it doesn't mention the manger. So it took a while for the wise men to travel to where Jesus was.
MR. MARTIN:	That's right. Some people think it could have been quite a few months before they found Him.
KATY:	And He had to wait all that time for His birthday gifts?
MR. MARTIN:	In a manner of speaking, Katy.
KATY:	Boy! I thought <u>I</u> had problems! *(start introduction to "Royal Gifts")*
MR. MARTIN:	Speaking of the wise men, if everyone is ready, let's rehearse that scene now . . . then we'll hear some of your birthday letters to Jesus.

(Katy has not written her letter yet; she slyly moves to one side of stage to write her letter during "Royal Gifts," after which she returns to her place on the risers.)

(Wise Men walk slowly down the aisle, looking around as if searching for something. As they walk, first verse and chorus of following song is sung.)

Royal Gifts

LINDA REBUCK

TOM FETTKE

*"We Three Kings of Orient Are" (John Hopkins.)

FM⁷ **G sus** **G** **Am⁷** **G⁷/B**

nize Him as King.

Slower ♩ = ca. 144

(45) **Cm** **Fm⁷/C** **G/B** **Cm** **Bb** **AbM⁷** (49) **Bb**

(Aaron, Michael, and Sarah enter.) SARAH: Look at those men, Father! They are dressed in such beautiful

mp

Cm **Bb** **Ab** **G** **Cm** (53) **Cm** **Bb**

robes. MICHAEL: They look important. AARON: Yes, they do! Do you remember the eastern kings

AbM⁷ **Gm** **Fm** **Gm** **AbM⁷** **Bb** **Ab⁶** **Cm/G** **G⁷** **Cm** **Bb⁷**

everyone has been talking about—the ones who are looking for the Christ-child? I wonder . . .

rit.

MICHAEL: Could we ask them? AARON: Well, I guess so . . . they seem to be coming this way. *(Wise men
come to where Michael, Aaron, and Sarah are standing. It is obvious that they are not sure where to go.)*
AARON: Hello. You appear to be lost. May I be of assistance?

(61) **Slower ♩ = ca. 126** (65)

Eb **Ab/Eb** **Eb** **Ab** **Gm** **Fm⁷** **Eb** **Ab/Eb**

FIRST KING: We have come a very long way seeking the newborn King of the Jews. We came to worship

Him and bring Him these gifts. SARAH: We saw Him! In a manger in Bethlehem. There were *thousands* of angels singing in the sky. Did you see them?

*The stop here is designated to give flexibility in the delivery of the preceeding dialogue from the standpoint of timing. The end of Sarah's line, "Did you see them?" should be close to the end of the music, but it need not be exact.

SECOND KING: No, but we have been following the star. *(to Aaron)* Sir, which way is Bethlehem?
AARON: Over that way. *(points over heads of audience)* THIRD KING: *(joyfully)* Look! Over Bethlehem! There's the star! Let's go. *(Other kings agree.)* Thank you, sir. *(Start tape after a short pause.)* *(They exit— aisle opposite the one they came down.)*

SARAH: Did you see the gifts they were carrying, Father? It looked like gold and perfume. My gift was so

small compared to theirs. AARON: Sarah, you gave the Baby Jesus your most important possession, and

that was very loving and unselfish. Besides, *we* are the ones receiving the gift. The Messiah is God's gift to

40

(93) the world. He is going to be our Savior. *(They exit or rejoin choir.)*

Dialogue should end here.

(99) a tempo ♩ = 184 (In one)

(103)

Gifts of the wise men, three

gifts of the wise men; Oh, what can these won-drous gifts be?

(111) One for His king-ship and one for His lord-ship And

42

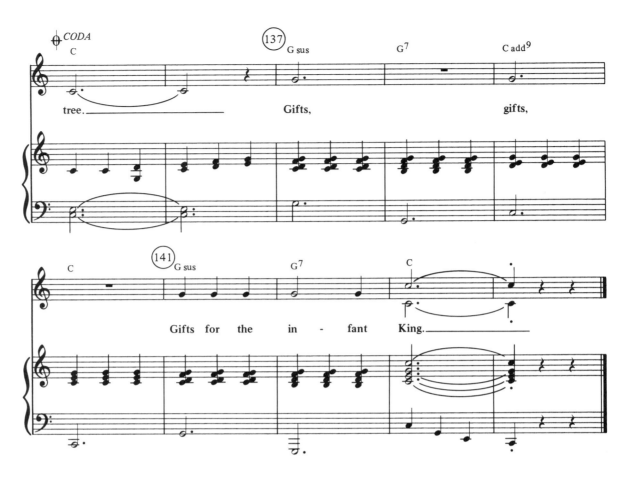

MR. MARTIN:	All right, boys and girls. That was great. Now, before we rehearse our last song, let's hear some of your birthday letters to Jesus. Who'd like to read one? *(Greg raises his hand.)* Okay, Greg.
GREG:	*(sniffing, always on the verge of a sneeze)* Dear Jesus, I don't know what to give You for Your birthday. Maybe I could give You my little sister. *(other kids laugh)* Just kidding. Happy birthday. Your friend, Greg.
MR. MARTIN:	Thank you, Greg. Would anyone else like to share a letter? *(more hands)* Jamie?
JAMIE:	Dear Jesus, happy birthday. Could You please help me find my watch? It's somewhere in my room, and You know what a mess <u>that</u> is! Thank You. Your friend, Jamie. P.S. I'm sorry about putting the lizard in Janet's purse.
MR. MARTIN:	That was good, Jamie. Let's hear one more letter. *(more hands)* Katy . . . would you like to read your letter?
KATY:	*(with a little bit of reluctance)* Dear Jesus, I wonder how <u>You</u> felt, growing up with Your birthday on Christmas. I've never had a party, but I'll bet You haven't either. I wonder if Christmas for You is just like it is for me . . . SPECTARAMAJINGAL-ICIOUSTINSELRIBBONISTMAS!
	(mumbles from other children, such as "What did she say?")
MR. MARTIN:	Hold on, Katy . . . what was that?
KATY:	SPECTARAMAJINGALICIOUSTINSELRIBBONISTMAS!
MR. MARTIN:	Specta . . . jingle. . . . What are you talking about?
KATY:	That's what Christmas has become! Spectaramajingalicioustinselribbonistmas!

SPECTARAMAJINGALICIOUS TINSELRIBBONISTMAS

(SPECTA-RAMA-JINGA-LICIOUS-TINSEL-RIBBON-ISTMAS)

LINDA REBUCK

TOM FETTKE

*May be sung by another soloist, or use full choir unison.

4-Part Round ending - optional

No accompaniment is provided—use measures 5 thru 12 of piano accompaniment if absolutely necessary.

I. Spec - ta - ra - ma - jin - gal - i - cious - tin - sel - rib - bon - ist - mas:

II. Things we do this time of year to take the place of Christ - mas.

III. It's a fact the birth - day of the King has some - how missed us.

IV. Spec - ta - ra - ma - jin - gal - i - cious - tin - sel - rib - bon - ist - mas.

The last line may be repeated by full choir after voice part IV has completed the line. Sing it with "gusto."

MR. MARTIN: That was <u>excellent</u>, Katy . . . I thought you were the one who felt left out at Christmas.

KATY: Yes, I did . . . but today I realized something . . . I didn't like Christmas because it kept me from getting a lot of gifts for my birthday; but <u>Jesus</u> is <u>God's</u> <u>Gift</u> to us, if we will just receive Him.

MR. MARTIN: Well, this should be your best birthday ever, Katy . . . you learned some very important lessons.

(One or two choir members go backstage momentarily and come back in carrying a birthday cake that says "Happy Birthday, Mary."

CHOIR: *(all together . . . brightly)* Happy birthday, Katy!

GREG: Uh-oh! The cake says, "Happy Birthday, <u>Mary</u>."

KATY: That's okay . . . Mary is a nice name . . . it was Jesus' mother's name. *(She looks at Mr. Martin and smiles.)* Thank you, everybody . . . but let's be sure we remember that it's <u>Jesus</u>' birthday, too.

MR. MARTIN: I hate to spoil your party, kids, but we have to clean up <u>everything</u> here for the Sunday morning church service. Let's get that done first, then you can go into the recreation room for cake.

Finale

including
On the Eve of the Pageant
Gettin' Ready for the Miracle

LINDA REBUCK

TOM FETTKE

Departure Music

On the Eve of the Pageant - Reprise

During this reprise, choir members go around taking down props and leave the stage a few at a time. Greg will be the last to leave as he renders one last sneeze at measure (38).

Based on Traditional English Folksong ,
"The Twelve Days of Christmas"
Arr. by Doug Holck and Tom Fettke

50